Reid

by Iain Gray

79 Main Street, Newtongrange,
Midlothian EH22 4NA
Tel: 0131 344 0414   Fax: 0845 075 6085
E-mail: info@lang-syne.co.uk
www.langsyneshop.co.uk

Design by Dorothy Meikle
Printed by Printwell Ltd
© Lang Syne Publishers Ltd 2019

All rights reserved. No part of this publication may be reproduced, stored or introduced into a retrieval system, or transmitted in any form or by any means (electronic, mechanical, photocopying, recording or otherwise) without the prior written permission of Lang Syne Publishers Ltd.

ISBN 978-1-85217-642-6

Reid

MOTTO:
Peace, plenty.

CREST:
A falcon.

NAME variations include:
- Read
- Reade
- Reed
- Reede
- Redd

Chapter one:

The origins of popular surnames

by George Forbes and Iain Gray

***If you don't know where you came from, you won't know where you're going** is a frequently quoted observation and one that has a particular resonance today when there has been a marked upsurge in interest in genealogy, with increasing numbers of people curious to trace their family roots.*

Main sources for genealogical research include census returns and official records of births, marriages and deaths – and the key to unlocking the detail they contain is obviously a family surname, one that has been 'inherited' and passed from generation to generation.

No matter our station in life, we all have a surname – but it was not until about the middle of the fourteenth century that the practice of being identified by a particular surname became commonly established throughout the British Isles.

Previous to this, it was normal for a person to be identified through the use of only a forename.

But as population gradually increased and there were many more people with the same forename, surnames were adopted to distinguish one person, or community, from another.

Many common English surnames are patronymic in origin, meaning they stem from the forename of one's father – with 'Johnson,' for example, indicating 'son of John.'

It was the Normans, in the wake of their eleventh century conquest of Anglo-Saxon England, a pivotal moment in the nation's history, who first brought surnames into usage – although it was a gradual process.

For the Normans, these were names initially based on the title of their estates, local villages and chateaux in France to distinguish and identify these landholdings.

Such grand descriptions also helped enhance the prestige of these warlords and generally glorify their lofty positions high above the humble serfs slaving away below in the pecking order who had only single names, often with Biblical connotations as in Pierre and Jacques.

The only descriptive distinctions among the peasantry concerned their occupations, like 'Pierre the swineherd' or 'Jacques the ferryman.'

Roots of surnames that came into usage in England not only included Norman-French, but also Old French, Old Norse, Old English, Middle English, German, Latin, Greek, Hebrew and the Gaelic languages of the Celts.

The Normans themselves were originally Vikings, or 'Northmen', who raided, colonised and eventually settled down around the French coastline.

The had sailed up the Seine in their longboats in 900AD under their ferocious leader Rollo and ruled the roost in north eastern France before sailing over to conquer England in 1066 under Duke William of Normandy – better known to posterity as William the Conqueror, or King William I of England.

Granted lands in the newly-conquered England, some of their descendants later acquired territories in Wales, Scotland and Ireland – taking not only their own surnames, but also the practice of adopting a surname, with them.

But it was in England where Norman rule and custom first impacted, particularly in relation to the adoption of surnames.

This is reflected in the famous *Domesday Book*, a massive survey of much of England and Wales, ordered by William I, to determine who owned what, what it was worth and therefore how much they were liable to pay in taxes to the voracious Royal Exchequer.

Completed in 1086 and now held in the National Archives in Kew, London, 'Domesday' was an Old English word meaning 'Day of Judgement.'

This was because, in the words of one contemporary chronicler, "its decisions, like those of the Last Judgement, are unalterable."

It had been a requirement of all those English landholders – from the richest to the poorest – that they identify themselves for the purposes of the survey and for future reference by means of a surname.

This is why the *Domesday Book*, although written in Latin as was the practice for several centuries with both civic and ecclesiastical records, is an invaluable source for the early appearance of a wide range of English surnames.

Several of these names were coined in connection with occupations.

These include Baker and Smith, while Cooks, Chamberlains, Constables and Porters were to be found carrying out duties in large medieval households.

The church's influence can be found in names such as Bishop, Friar and Monk while the popular name of Bennett derives from the late fifth to mid-sixth century Saint Benedict, founder of the Benedictine order of monks.

The early medical profession is represented by Barber, while businessmen produced names that include Merchant and Sellers.

Down at the village watermill, the names that cropped up included Millar/Miller, Walker and Fuller, while other self-explanatory trades included Cooper, Tailor, Mason and Wright.

Even the scenery was utilised as in Moor, Hill, Wood and Forrest – while the hunt and the chase supplied names that include Hunter, Falconer, Fowler and Fox.

Colours are also a source of popular surnames, as in Black, Brown, Gray/Grey, Green and White, and would have denoted the colour of the clothing the person habitually wore or, apart from the obvious exception of 'Green', one's hair colouring or even complexion.

The surname Red developed into Reid, while

Blue was rare and no-one wanted to be associated with yellow.

Rather self-important individuals took surnames that include Goodman and Wiseman, while physical attributes crept into surnames such as Small and Little.

Many families proudly boast the heraldic device known as a Coat of Arms, as featured on our front cover.

The central motif of the Coat of Arms would originally have been what was borne on the shield of a warrior to distinguish himself from others on the battlefield.

Not featured on the Coat of Arms, but highlighted on page three, is the family motto and related crest – with the latter frequently different from the central motif.

Adding further variety to the rich cultural heritage that is represented by surnames is the appearance in recent times in lists of the 100 most common names found in England of ones that include Khan, Patel and Singh – names that have proud roots in the vast sub-continent of India.

Echoes of a far distant past can still be found in our surnames and they can be borne with pride in commemoration of our forebears.

Chapter two:

Ancient roots

A name with a number of possible points of origin, 'Reid' and its popular spelling variants that include 'Read' and 'Reed', has roots that lie deeply buried in the ancient soil of England.

Ranked at 75th in some lists of the 100 most common surnames found in England today and also prevalent throughout Scotland, Northern Ireland and the Irish Republic, one derivation is from the Old English 'read', meaning 'red', and would have been used as a nickname for someone with red hair or of a ruddy complexion.

As a forename, it would have originally appeared as 'Rufus' while another point of origin, this time topographical, is from the Old English 'ryd' or 'reid', indicating someone who lived in a woodland clearing.

Meanwhile as a locational surname it has links with, for example, Reed in Hertfordshire, Rede in Suffolk and Read in Lancashire.

Concerning the derivation of what became the Reid surname as descriptive of someone with red hair or of a ruddy complexion, some sources suggest it may have been a term for the early Anglo-Saxons, many of whom were distinguished by their flame-red hair.

This, in addition to the fact that the name pre-dates by several centuries the Norman Conquest of 1066, means that flowing through the veins of many bearers of the name today may well be the blood of those Germanic tribes who invaded and settled in the south and east of the island of Britain from about the early fifth century.

Known as the Anglo-Saxons, they were composed of the Jutes, from the area of the Jutland Peninsula in modern Denmark, the Saxons from Lower Saxony, in modern Germany and the Angles from the Angeln area of Germany.

It was the Angles who gave the name 'Engla land', or 'Aengla land' – better known as 'England.'

They held sway in what became England from approximately 550 to 1066, with the main kingdoms those of Sussex, Wessex, Northumbria, Mercia, Kent, East Anglia and Essex.

Whoever controlled the most powerful of these kingdoms was tacitly recognised as overall 'king' – one of the most noted being Alfred the Great, King of Wessex from 871 to 899.

It was during his reign that the famous *Anglo-Saxon Chronicle* was compiled – an invaluable source of Anglo-Saxon history – while Alfred was designated in early documents as *Rex Anglorum Saxonum*, King of the English Saxons.

Other important Anglo-Saxon works include the epic *Beowulf* and the seventh century *Caedmon's Hymn*.

Through the Anglo-Saxons, the language known as Old English developed, later transforming from the eleventh century into Middle English – sources from which many popular English surnames of today, such as Reid, derive.

The Anglo-Saxons meanwhile, had usurped the power of the indigenous Britons – who referred to them as 'Saeson' or 'Saxones.'

It is from this that the Scottish Gaelic term for 'English people' of 'Sasannach' derives, the Irish Gaelic 'Sasanach' and the Welsh 'Saeson.'

We learn from the *Anglo-Saxon Chronicle* how the religion of the early Anglo-Saxons was one that pre-dated the establishment of Christianity in the British Isles.

Known as a form of Germanic paganism, with roots in Old Norse religion, it shared much in common with the Druidic 'nature-worshipping' religion of the indigenous Britons.

It was in the closing years of the sixth century that Christianity began to take a hold in Britain, while by approximately 690 it had become the 'established' religion of Anglo-Saxon England.

The death knell of Anglo-Saxon supremacy was sounded with the Norman Conquest of 1066 – a pivotal event in England's history.

By this date, it had become a nation with several powerful competitors to the throne.

In what were extremely complex family, political and military machinations, the monarch was Harold II, who had succeeded to the throne following the death of Edward the Confessor.

But his right to the throne was contested by two powerful competitors – his brother-in-law King Harold Hardrada of Norway, in alliance with Tostig, Harold II's brother, and Duke William II of Normandy.

In what has become known as The Year of Three Battles, Hardrada invaded England and gained victory over the English king on September 20 at the battle of Fulford, in Yorkshire.

Five days later, however, Harold II decisively defeated his brother-in-law and brother at the battle of Stamford Bridge.

But he had little time to celebrate his victory, having to immediately march south from Yorkshire to encounter a mighty invasion force led by Duke William that had landed at Hastings, in East Sussex.

Harold's battle-hardened but exhausted force confronted the Normans on October 14, drawing up a strong defensive position at the top of Senlac Hill, building a shield wall to repel William's cavalry and infantry.

The Normans suffered heavy losses, but through a combination of the deadly skill of their archers and the ferocious determination of their cavalry they eventually won the day.

Morale had collapsed on the battlefield as word spread through the ranks that Harold, the last of the Anglo-Saxon kings, had been slain.

William was declared King of England on December 25, and the complete subjugation of his Anglo-Saxon subjects followed, with those Normans who had fought on his behalf rewarded with the lands of Anglo-Saxons, many of whom sought exile abroad as mercenaries.

Within an astonishingly short space of time, Norman manners, customs and law were imposed on England – laying the basis for what subsequently became established 'English' custom and practice.

But beneath the surface, old Anglo-Saxon culture was not totally eradicated, with some aspects absorbed into those of the Normans, while faint echoes of the Anglo-Saxon past is still seen today in the form of popular surnames such as Reid.

The Reids came to be particularly associated with Northumberland, in the far north of England, while many bearers of the name throughout the British Isles came to figure prominently in the colourful and frequently turbulent drama that is the island's historical record.

Involved in discussing peace terms on behalf of his nation with England's Henry VIII, for example, Robert Reid was the Scottish abbot who, on his death in 1558 left substantial funds that led to the foundation of what is now the centre of academic excellence known as the University of Edinburgh.

Chapter three:

Fame and infamy

One particularly colourful bearer of the Reid name was the British First World War flying ace and Conservative Party politician Alex Stratford Reid.

Born in 1895 in Wayland, Suffolk, the son of a clergyman and later to style himself Alex Stratford Cunningham-Reid, he served during the 1914 to 1918 conflict with the Royal Engineers before transferring to the Royal Flying Corps (RFC), forerunner of the Royal Air Force (RAF).

It was in August of 1918 that Captain Cunningham-Reid was awarded the Distinguished Flying Cross after attacking and burning down an enemy reconnaissance balloon and over the following three days engaging and shooting down three enemy aircraft.

Entering politics in 1922 as Conservative Member of Parliament (MP) for Warrington, it was 21 years later, in July of 1943 and after having served in a number of other constituencies, that he was at the centre of an infamous incident that made press headlines.

This was when he was involved in an

exchange of blows in the lobby of the Commons with fellow Conservative MP Oliver Locker-Lampson – who had apparently accused him of deliberately having left London during the devastating Luftwaffe bombing blitz on the capital in 1940.

Cunningham-Reid had retorted that he had actually left London on a planned 14-week trip before the blitz had started, and the pair resorted to an unseemly exchange of fisticuffs.

Both MPs had to make a formal apology to the Commons, while Cunningham-Reid was reported in the press as stating: "He (Locker-Lampson) ran whirling his arms around his head and struck me in the chest.

"I retaliated by hitting him on the head. He went down on his knees. I helped him up, and by that time other members had gotten between us."

He was married twice, firstly to the Honourable Ruth Mary Clarisse Ashley, daughter of the multi-millionaire Colonel Wilfred Ashley, 1st Baron Mount Temple, and at the time of their wedding in 1927 the couple were described as "England's wealthiest girl and handsomest man."

They divorced in 1940, while during the war he conducted an affair with the American heiress and socialite Doris Duke.

Daughter of a wealthy tobacco tycoon and rarely out of the gossip columns, she also became noted as an art collector, horticulturist and philanthropist – with the bulk of her fortune, estimated at a staggering $1.3 billion, left to a range of charitable causes following her death in 1993, aged 81.

Married from 1944 to 1949 to Angela Williams, Cunninghame-Reid died in 1977 in Valbonne, France.

In common with Cunninghame-Reid, Ellis Vair Reid was also a First World War flying ace.

Born in 1889 in Belleville, Ontario, the Canadian pilot was awarded the Distinguished Service Cross after attacking and destroying four enemy aircraft over the Western Front in June of 1918 – but he was reported missing in action only a few weeks later.

Also taking to the skies, Wilfred Reid, born in Surrey in 1887, was the English aircraft designer recognised today as one of the pioneers of the Canadian aircraft industry.

Working during the First World War for the Bristol Aeroplane Company, he helped to design aircraft that included the Braemar Bomber and the Bristol M.R.I. while after taking over as the company's chief designer in 1921, he designed the Bristol Racer, the Berkeley and the Bloodhound.

Appointed chief aircraft designer for Canadian Vickers Ltd. in 1924, and later forming his own company, Reid Aircraft, he was responsible for the Vickers Vedette and a number of other aircraft.

The company was bought in 1928 by Curtiss Aeroplane and Motor Company to form the Curtiss-Reid Aircraft Company, makers of the Curtiss-Reid Rambler light training aeroplane.

An inductee of the Quebec Air and Space Hall of Fame, the visionary Reid died in 1968, while in 1994 the Royal Canadian Mint issued a $20 coin honouring him and his creation the Vickers Vedette.

During the Second World War, Patrick Robert Reid, better known as Pat Reid, gained fame as one of the escapees from what was considered the 'escape-proof' fortress of Colditz Castle, in Germany.

Born in India in 1910 and of Irish parentage, he had worked before the outbreak of the war in September of 1939 as a civil engineer, becoming an associate member of the Institution of Civil Engineers in 1936.

Having joined the Territorial Army, he was mobilised for active service and it was while serving in the 2nd Infantry Division, with the rank of temporary captain, that he was captured in May of 1940 during the German onslaught on France.

Sent as a prisoner-of-war to Laufen Castle in Bavaria, officially designated Oflag VII-C, in September of 1940 Reid and five others managed to escape after constructing a tunnel that led from the prison's basement to a shed that adjoined a nearby house. Against all the odds, they remained on the loose for five days before being recaptured in Radstadt, Austria.

Sent to Colditz Castle, designated Oflag-IV-C, Reid made another attempt at escape in May of 1941, only to be thwarted, while in October of the following year he and four others managed a successful escape, arriving in neutral Switzerland – with Reid having adopted the guise of a Flemish worker – after five days.

Their daring and meticulously planned escape had involved cutting through the bars on a window in the prisoners' kitchen, crawling through an air shaft that led from a storage cellar to the castle moat and, from there, across a park and on their way to freedom.

Remaining in Switzerland until the end of the war, working for the British Secret Intelligence

Service (SIS), Reid was later awarded the Military Cross and the honorary rank of major and also made an MBE.

Returning to his pre-war career in civil engineering, he died in 1990, while his 1952 book *The Colditz Story* formed the basis three years later of the film of the name, with John Mills portraying the indomitable Reid.

In the world of politics, James Reid, better known as Jimmy Reid, born in Govan, Glasgow, in 1932, was the Scottish trade union activist, politician, orator and journalist particularly noted for his leadership, along with others who included Jimmy Airlie, of the 'work-in' to save the Upper Clyde Shipbuilders (UCS) yard, on the Clyde, in the early 1970s.

The campaign, which attracted international media attention and messages of support from celebrities including John Lennon and Yoko Ono, was successful and the former engineer by trade – who in his lifetime embraced political parties that included the Communist Party, the Labour Party and the Scottish National Party – was hailed as a hero of the working class.

Elected rector of Glasgow University in 1971, he delivered an impassioned acceptance speech that

The *New York Times* described as "the greatest speech since Lincoln's Gettysburg Address."

Delivered in high and inspiring oratorical style, part of the speech contained the observation: "A rat race is for rats. We're not rats. We're human beings.

"Reject the insidious pressures in society that could blunt your critical faculties to all that is happening around you, that would caution silence in the face of injustice lest you jeopardise your chances of promotion and self-advancement …"

Latterly a journalist and broadcaster, he died in 2010, while the think-tank and advocacy group *The Jimmy Reid Foundation* was established in his memory by the editorial board of *Scottish Left Review*.

Having held high office in a number of British government posts, John Reid, also known as Dr John Reid and more formally as Baron Reid of Cardowan, is the Labour Party politician whose Cabinet posts included Health Secretary, Secretary of State for Scotland, Secretary of State for Northern Ireland, Defence Secretary and, from 2006 to 2007, Home Secretary.

Born in 1947 in Bellshill, North Lanarkshire, he worked for a time as a researcher for the Labour Party before being elected MP for Motherwell North in 1987. It was when he was aged in his mid-20s that he gained a degree in history and later a Ph.D. in economic history – hence his title of Dr John Reid.

Standing down as an MP in 2010 and being elevated to the House of Lords as Baron Reid of Cardowan, he also served from 2007 to 2011 as chairman of Celtic Football Club.

One particularly infamous bearer of the otherwise proud name of Reid is the convicted terrorist Richard Reid – otherwise known as the "Shoe Bomber."

Born in 1973 in Bromley, London, and having converted to Islam as a young man while serving time in prison for petty criminal offences, he later travelled to Pakistan and Afghanistan after becoming 'radicalised' and where he trained with and became a member of Al-Qaeda.

It was in December of 2001, wearing shoes packed with explosives, that he boarded American Airlines Flight 63 in Paris, bound for Miami. After unsuccessfully trying to detonate the explosives and being subdued by fellow passengers, he was tried and convicted in an American court in 2002 of eight criminal counts of terrorism and sentenced to three life terms plus 110 years in prison without parole.

Chapter four:

On the world stage

The recipient of three Grammy Awards, Antonio M."L.A." Reid is the American musician, songwriter, producer and record company executive born in Cincinnati in 1956.

Recognised for his drumming skills, he has worked with artists who include Mariah Carey, Paula Abdul, Justin Bieber, Rihanna and Kanye West, while he also appeared as a judge on the first two seasons of the American version of the television musical talent show *The X Factor*.

Chairman and chief executive of Epic Records, in 2013 he was a recipient of the National Academy of Recording Arts and Science's President's Merit Award in recognition of his contribution to the music industry.

Born in Leith in 1962, **Charlie** and **Craig Reid** are the Scottish identical twin brothers who, since 1983, have enjoyed international success with their band The Proclaimers.

Hit singles include *Letter from America*, *I'm on My Way* and *I'm Gonna Be (500 miles)* – with the latter re-recorded in 2007 and featuring a host of celebrities in an accompanying music video to raise money for the Comic Relief charity.

A stage musical featuring their songs, *Sunshine on Leith*, was created in 2007 and adapted for a film of the name six years later.

Also in Scotland, **Alan Reid**, born in Glasgow in 1950, is the multi-instrumentalist and songwriter who in 1969 was one of the founding members of the folk group Battlefield Band.

With the band until 2010, he now forms part of a musical duo along with Battlefield Band's former sound engineer Rob van Sante.

On the stage, **Tara Donna Reid** is the American actress and model whose many film credits include, when aged 12, *A Return to Salem's Lot*, the 1998 *The Big Lebowski*, the 1999 *American Pie* and, from 2014, *Sharknado*.

Born in Wyckoff, New Jersey in 1975, her television credits include *Days of Our Lives*, *California Dreams* and *Scrubs*.

Known as "the screen's most perfect lover", William Wallace Halleck Reid was the American actor and producer of the silent film era better known as **Wallace Reid**.

Born in St Louis, Missouri in 1891, the son of the actress Bertha Westbrook and the actor and playwright Hal Reid, his movie debut was in the 1910 *The Phoenix*, while other major credits that made him a Hollywood heartthrob – starring beside leading ladies such as Gloria Swanson and Lillian Gish – include the 1915 *Birth of a Nation*, the 1916 *Intolerance* the 1921 *Too Much Speed* and, from 1922, *Across the Continent*.

Becoming addicted to morphine after being badly injured in a train crash in 1919 while on location in Oregon for the filming of *The Valley of the Giants*, he died in 1923, while he is the recipient of a star on the Hollywood Walk of Fame.

His 2011 biography *Wally: The True Wallace Reid Story*, by David W. Menefee, was nominated for a Pulitzer Prize.

Born in 1914 in Wichita Falls, Texas, Anna May Priest was the American actress of stage, television and film better known as **Frances Reid**.

Making her Broadway debut in 1939 in *Where There's a Will There's a Way*, her television credits include *Perry Mason*, *As the World Turns* and *Days of Our Lives*.

With other credits that include appearing

opposite Rock Hudson in the 1966 drama *Seconds* and the recipient in 2004 of a Daytime Lifetime Achievement Award, she died in 2010.

Known for her role from 1993 until 1996 in the television sitcom *The Fresh Prince of Bel-Air*, starring opposite Will Smith, **Daphne Maxwell Reid** is the American actress and former model born in New York City in 1948.

With other television credits that include *Murder, She Wrote*, she is married to the actor, comedian and film director **Tim Reid**, born in 1944 and whose television credits include *Venus Flytrap* and, from 2004 to 2006, *That '70s Show*.

Made a Member of the Order of Canada in 2006, **Fiona Reid** is the English-born Canadian actress of stage, television and film noted for her role of Cathy in the television series *King of Kensington*.

Born in 1951 in Whitstable, Kent and later immigrating with her family to Canada, she is also the recipient of two Dora Mavor Moore Awards; these were in 1993 for *Fallen Angels* and, two years later, for *Six Degrees of Separation*.

On British shores, **James Reid** was the Scottish actor born in 1939 in Hamilton, Lanarkshire. Graduating from the Royal Scottish Academy of Music and Drama in 1962 and a recipient of its Silver Medal for Acting, he went on to gain credits for roles in television series that include *Doctor Finlay*, *Peak Practice*, *Taggart* and *Lovejoy*.

As a stage actor, it was in 2003 that, midway through a performance in the role of Vladimir in Samuel Beckett's *Waiting for Godot*, at the Finsborough Theatre in London's Earls Court, that he collapsed and died on stage.

Best known for his role as host of the popular British television show *Runaround* and as Frank Butcher in the soap *EastEnders*, **Mike Reid** was the English comedian and actor born in London in 1940.

One of the stars, as a stand-up comedian, in the 1970s' television series *The Comedians* and having appeared in other television soaps that include *The Bill*, he died in 2007.

Born in Penzance in 1980, **Alex Reid** is the English actress whose television credits include *Misfits*, *Life on Mars* and *Ultimate Force*.

Bearers of the Reid name have also excelled in the highly competitive world of sport.

Born in 1975 in Aldershot, Hampshire, Alexander Aristides Reid, better known as **Alex Reid**, is the English martial artist, kickboxer and actor nicknamed "Reidernator."

The winner in 2010 of the British television show *Celebrity Big Brother*, he was married for a time to the celebrity and former glamour model Katie Price.

On the cricket pitch, **John Reid**, born in 1956 in Auckland, is the New Zealand cricketer who between 1979 and 1986 played in 25 One Day Internationals and 19 Tests.

He is a cousin of the Australian former cricketer **Bruce Reid**, born in 1963 and who represented his nation in Test matches between 1985 and 1992 and who has also been a bowling coach for the Indian national team.

In the boxing ring, **David Reid**, nicknamed "The American Dream", is the American former boxer, born in Philadelphia in 1973, who won a gold medal in the Light Middleweight event at the 1996 Olympic Games.

In the swimming pool, **Jamie Reid**, born in 1983 in Payullup, Washington, is the American former backstroke competitor who won the gold medal in the women's 100-metres event at the 2003 Pan American Games.

From swimming to golf, **Michael Reid**, born

in 1954 in Bainbridge, Maryland, is the American player who, after taking up the golf clubs at the tender age of five, has gone on to win two senior majors on the Champions Tour and two Professional Golf Association (PGA) Tour events.

On the fields of European football, **Andy Reid**, born in Dublin in 1982, is the Irish midfielder who, in addition to playing for his national team, has played for clubs that include Nottingham Forest, Tottenham, Charlton Athletic, Sunderland and Blackpool.

From sport to the creative world of the written word, **Christopher Reid** is the award-winning British poet, writer, essayist and cartoonist born in Hong Kong in 1949.

Winner in 2009 of the Costa Book Award for *A Scattering* and having worked as poetry editor for publishing house Faber and Faber, his other acclaimed works include his 1996 *Two Dogs on a Pub Roof* and, from 2012, *Nonsense*.

Regarded as one of Northern Ireland's greatest novelists, **Forrest Reid**, born in Belfast in 1875, was the writer, literary critic and translator whose novel *Young Tom* won him the 1944 James Black Tait Memorial Prize.

Having written other acclaimed works that include his 1912 novel *Following Darkness*, he died in 1947.

From literature to the equally creative world of art, **Robert Lewis Reid** was the American Impressionist painter and muralist whose many works to this day grace the Congressional Library in Washington, D.C., and the State House in Boston – most notably his *Boston Tea Party* and *Paul Revere's Ride*.

Originally a member of the elite group of artists known as Ten American Painters, and who seceded in 1906 from the Society of American Artists in favour of the National Academy of Design, Reid, born in 1862 in Stockbridge, Massachusetts, died in 1929.

In the highly cerebral world of mathematics, **Constance Bowman Reid**, born in 1918 in St Louis, Missouri, is recognised as having popularised the subject of mathematics by explaining it in lay person's terms.

Although not a mathematician herself, it was as a freelance writer that she turned her attention to mathematics, penning best-selling books that include her 1959 *Introduction to Higher Mathematics*, her 1963 *A Long Way from Euclid* and *Men of Mathematics*, a collection of biographies of famous mathematicians.

Married in 1950 to the lawyer Neil D. Reid, she died in 2010 – four years after the publication of her *Julia: A Life in Mathematics*.

This was a biography of her sister Julia Hall Bowman Robinson, born in 1919 and who was the first woman to be appointed, two years before her death in 1985, President of the American Mathematical Society; she had been married to Raphael Robinson, also a noted mathematician.

On a murderous note, **Paul Dennis Reid, Jr.**, born in 1957 in Richland Hills, Texas, was the American serial killer known as "The Fast Food Killer".

It was while on parole from a conviction for aggravated robbery at a steakhouse that, between February and April of 1997, he killed a total of seven employees in the course of robbing three separate fast food restaurants, in Nashville, Tennessee and Clarksville, Tennessee.

Sentenced to death, he died in hospital in 2013 before the sentence could be carried out.